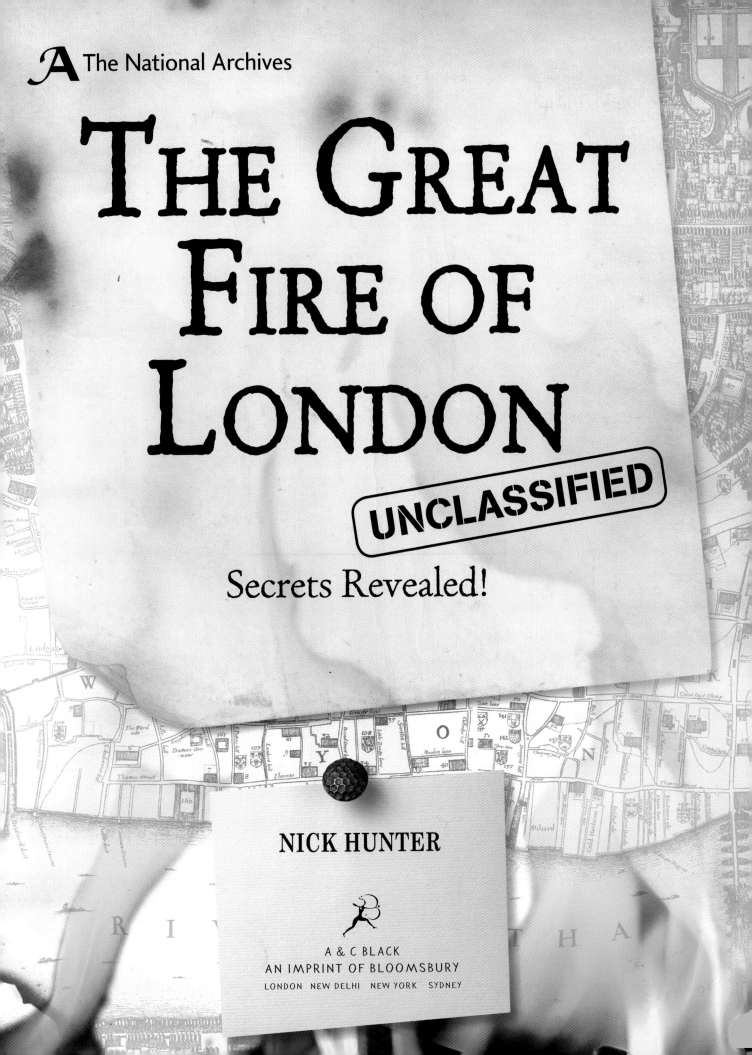

A The National Archives

THE GREAT FIRE OF LONDON

UNCLASSIFIED

Secrets Revealed!

NICK HUNTER

A & C BLACK

AN IMPRINT OF BLOOMSBURY

LONDON   NEW DELHI   NEW YORK   SYDNEY

Published 2013 by A & C Black,
an imprint of Bloomsbury Publishing Plc,
50 Bedford Square
London, WC1B 3DP

www.bloomsbury.com

Design by Nick Avery Design

ISBN: 978-1-4081-9303-7

A CIP catalogue for this book is available from the British Library.

CONTENTS

CITY IN RUINS

On the morning of 7 September 1666, John Evelyn struggled across mountains of burning ash. He took care to avoid the holes and cellars in the ground where houses and shops had once stood. The smoking remains of London stretched as far as he could see.

Evelyn was amazed by the destruction of the great buildings he knew so well. St Paul's Cathedral and the Royal Exchange lay in ruins. Beyond the smouldering city he met thousands of homeless families, carrying all of the belongings they had managed to save.

Rising from the ashes?

The great city of London had been destroyed by a huge fire. Evelyn and the people of London must have all been asking themselves the same questions. How could they rebuild their lives in this shattered city, and would London ever rise again?

▲ John Evelyn recorded his experience of the fire in his famous diary.

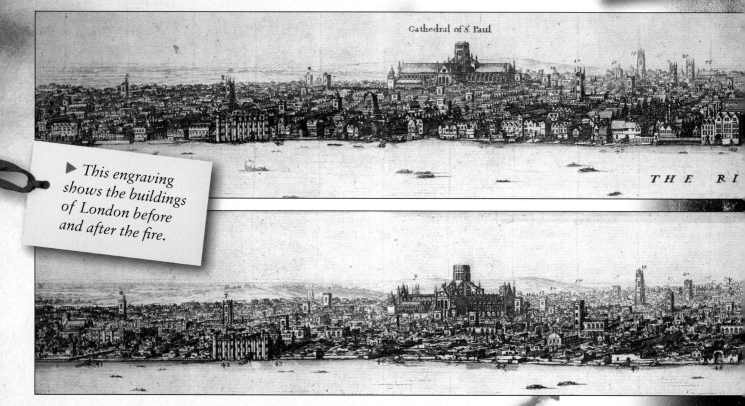

Cathedral of S. Paul

THE RI

▶ This engraving shows the buildings of London before and after the fire.

John Evelyn described the ruins of his city in his diary on 7 September 1666:

"I went this morning on foot from Whitehall as far as London Bridge . . . clambering over mountains of yet smoking rubbish, and frequently mistaking where I was. The lanes and narrower streets were quite filled up with rubbish, nor could one have possibly known where he was, but by the ruins of some church, or hall . . ."

John Evelyn

▲ Londoners watched their burning city from the safety of the River Thames.

THE CITY BY THE THAMES

Visitors to London during the 1660s were impressed by the large and wealthy city. In fact, London was three separate cities. The city of Westminster was the home of the king and parliament. South of the River Thames was the rough and rowdy city of Southwark. And across London Bridge from Southwark, on the north side of the river, was the city of London itself: a bustling, chaotic centre of trade and commerce.

The buildings of London came right down to the banks of the River Thames. One visitor believed there were as many as 2,000 ships of all shapes and sizes on the river at any one time. The ships brought riches to the city of London, as well as goods and people from around the world.

Streets of London

Londoners in 1666 would not have recognized the broad streets and grand stone buildings of modern London. The streets of the city were often narrow and packed with buildings that jutted out over the streets until they were almost touching the other side.

▶ Londoners lived in narrow twisting streets before the Great Fire.

▼ Spacious squares like the new Covent Garden in Westminster were very different from the cramped and smelly streets of old London.

6

French visitor Samuel Sorbière was amazed by the size of London. After visiting the city in 1663, he wrote:

"It requires a year's time to live in it before you have a very exact idea of the place."

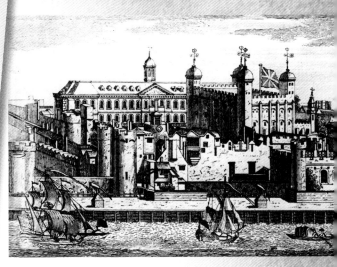

▲ *The Tower of London in the east was London's fortress against attack.*

Fire facts

London in 1666 was home to around 350,000 people and growing fast. At least one in six people from England lived in London at some point during their lives.

Old London. 1642.

LIVING IN FEAR

The bustle and noise of London in 1666 disguised the fact that the city had been through some difficult times. Many people listened to the predictions of astrologers and other mystics who claimed they could see into the future. They all said that 1666 would be an unlucky year. Londoners thought they'd had enough bad luck already.

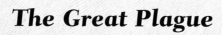
▲ Mystics and madmen predicted doom for London.

City at war

London had been at the centre of the English Civil War, which had been fought between supporters of King Charles I and parliament. The King had been executed on the streets of London in 1649, and many religious people believed that God would punish Londoners for beheading him. Although his son, King Charles II, had been crowned in 1660, things were still tense between the two sides.

King Charles II

The English Civil War may have been over, but by 1665, the English were once again at war with the Dutch. People living in the bustling port of London also feared attacks from France and Spain.

The Great Plague

Then in 1665, London was hit by a terrible plague. The disease killed as many as 100,000 Londoners in just a few months. Plague was still raging across England, and no one knew if it would strike the city again in the hot, dry summer of 1666.

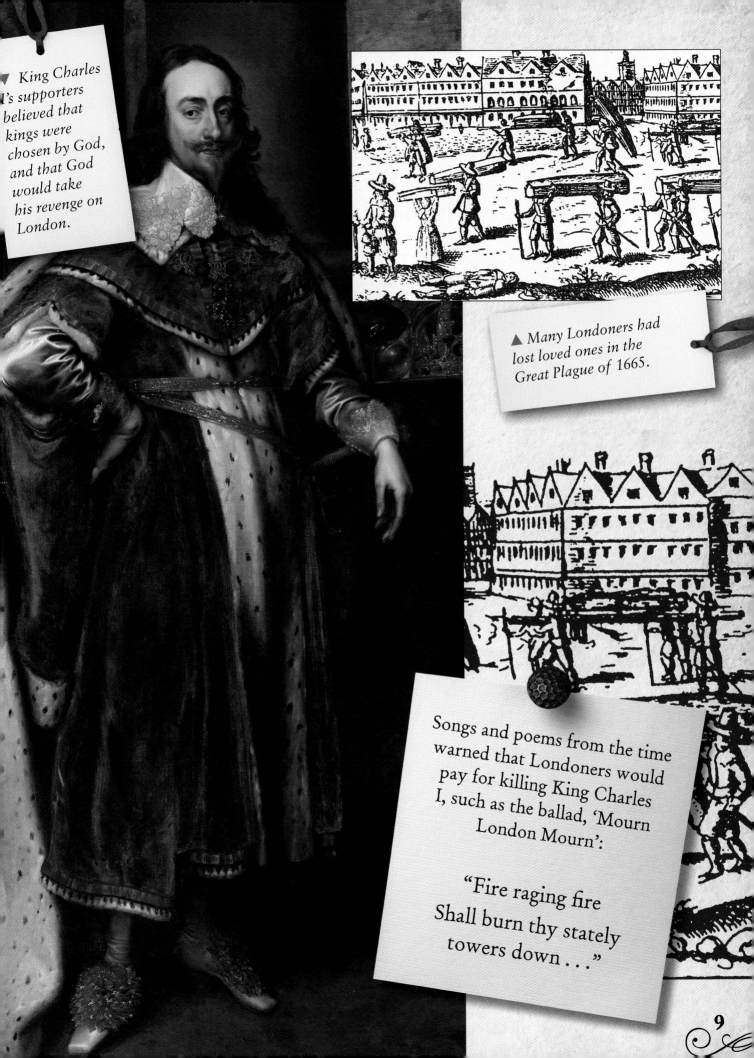

King Charles I's supporters believed that kings were chosen by God, and that God would take his revenge on London.

▲ Many Londoners had lost loved ones in the Great Plague of 1665.

Songs and poems from the time warned that Londoners would pay for killing King Charles I, such as the ballad, 'Mourn London Mourn':

"Fire raging fire
Shall burn thy stately
towers down . . ."

FEAR OF FIRE

London, like most European cities at the time, was mainly built of wood, which burns easily. There were few rules about new buildings, so wood-framed houses and shops were crammed tightly together. Candles were the main way of lighting buildings and open fires were the only way of cooking or heating. It is no wonder that most people who lived in cities lived in constant fear of fire.

▼ *An untended candle could easily start a major fire.*

▲ *London was destroyed by fire just a few years after the Romans founded the city.*

London's first fire

Sometimes fires were started deliberately. London was first destroyed by fire in AD 60, not long after Roman invaders had first founded the city. Queen Boudica, leader of the Iceni tribe, led a revolt against the Romans that included burning the Romans' new city, "Londinium", to the ground.

Deadly explosions had also rocked London in the past. In 1650, several barrels of gunpowder exploded accidentally in a shop, destroying many houses and starting a fierce fire. After that, the city introduced strict new rules about the storage of gunpowder.

▼ *Gunpowder was used on ships leaving the River Thames and was stored in many of London's buildings.*

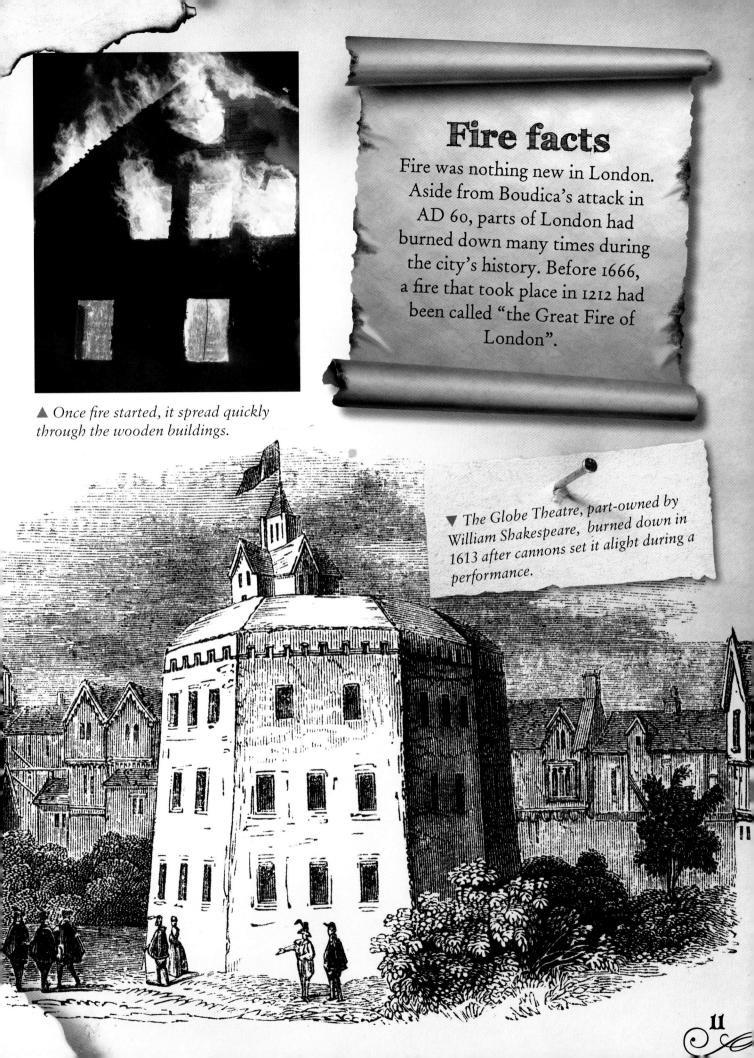

Fire facts

Fire was nothing new in London. Aside from Boudica's attack in AD 60, parts of London had burned down many times during the city's history. Before 1666, a fire that took place in 1212 had been called "the Great Fire of London".

▲ Once fire started, it spread quickly through the wooden buildings.

▼ The Globe Theatre, part-owned by William Shakespeare, burned down in 1613 after cannons set it alight during a performance.

FIRE WARNING

If a fire broke out in the city, there was no fire brigade to call for help. Each parish was expected to have its own equipment for fighting fires, and everyone who lived in the parish was expected to help stop the fire before it spread. People knew that if a fire burned out of control, their own homes and businesses could be destroyed.

Fire equipment included buckets, which would be filled in the River Thames and then passed along a line of people to reach the fire. Fire squirts, which were metal tubes that sucked up and squirted out water, were also used to try and put out fires. Buckets and squirts might put out a small fire, but they were no match for a major blaze.

The last resort

The only solution for a major fire was to destroy the buildings in its path. Wooden buildings would be pulled down with fire hooks and axes so the fire would have nothing to burn.

▶ This leather fire bucket dates from 1660 and was found close to where the Great Fire started.

These Engins.(which are ___ the best)to quinch great Fires,are
JOHN KEELING Fec.

▲ *Apart from having wheels, this fire engine is similar to the ones used in London in 1666.*

▲ The wealthy city livery companies provided money for London's basic fire defences.

Fetch the engines!

In 1666, fire engines had only recently been invented. The people that made them claimed the engines could do the same job as 500 people with buckets. A seventeenth century fire engine was basically a large container of water with a pipe for pumping water on to the fire. It was carried on a large sledge that had to be dragged through the streets by a team of men or horses.

Fire facts

In 1642, London's Lord Mayor asked the major city livery companies of trades and craftspeople to each pay £35 for a fire engine to protect the city.

▼ The fire equipment of the time was not powerful enough to protect the huge city of London.

FLUVIUS   THE BRIDGE   warke

PANIC ON PUDDING LANE

On the night of 1 September 1666, Thomas Farriner, his daughter Hanna, and two servants went to bed after a hard day at work in their bakery. The bakery was on Pudding Lane, close to London Bridge. Farriner later said that he was certain the fire in his oven was out.

Fire!

At one o'clock in the morning on Sunday 2 September, Farriner's servant discovered a fire in the bakery and raised the alarm. The fire was so fierce that Farriner and the others could not leave by the front door. Instead they made their escape across the rooftops of neighbouring houses. Farriner's maid was too scared to go with them, and sadly became the first victim of the fire.

The baker's neighbours on Pudding Lane were soon awake. They rushed into the street to try and put out the fire with buckets of water and anything else they could find. For an hour they battled to stop the fire spreading from the bakery but the flames were too strong. The parish constables were called – this fire looked serious.

▶ *London's bread had to be freshly baked every day in ovens like the one in Thomas Farriner's bakery.*

▼ As the fire spread along the street, neighbours would have helped to fight it. They had little chance of success.

▲ Pudding Lane was close to the northern end of London Bridge. This was the only way across the River Thames and was lined with buildings.

▶ This is a list of all the people who lived in Pudding lane and how many fireplaces they had. They had to pay a tax for each fireplace. Thomas Farriner is listed as owning five fireplaces and one oven.

THE FIRE SPREADS

There had been no rain in London for many weeks. The wooden buildings were bone dry and the flames were fanned by a strong wind from the east. These were perfect conditions for the fire to spread.

The riverbank close to Pudding Lane was lined with warehouses packed full of materials such as oils, paper, and tar, which would burn easily. When the sun came up on Sunday morning, the fire was already spreading down the hill towards London Bridge.

By early Sunday morning, the fire had already destroyed hundreds of houses but most Londoners were not too alarmed. After all, fires like this were not unusual. However, by mid-morning, word of the fire had spread. Schoolboy William Taswell was at Westminster Abbey when he first heard of a great fire in the city. Londoners started to worry. How could this fire be stopped?

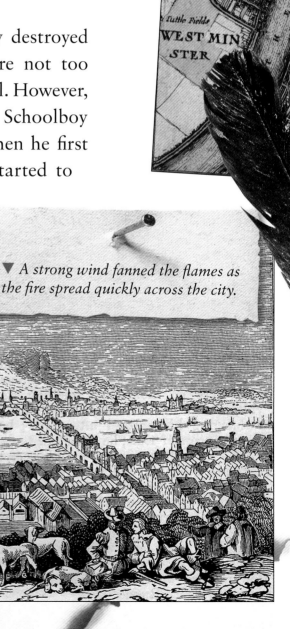

▼ A strong wind fanned the flames as the fire spread quickly across the city.

LONDON

Pudding Lane

1 S. Paul
2 Christ Church Coy.
3 Smithfield,
4 Charterhouse yard,
5 S. Iohns,
6 Clarkenwell greene,
7 Hatton garden,
8 Clarkenwell bridewell,
9 Aldersgate Street,
10 Old Street,
11 Artilerie Yard,

18 Aldgate,
19 Tower hill,
20 East Smithfield,
21 The Minories,
22 Custome house,

29 Queene hythe,
50 Paules wharffe,
31 Blackfriers Staires,
32 Whitfriers Staires,
33 Temple Staires,

Stepney

SOVTHWARKE

S. Georges Fields

Redriff

Scale of Miles

34 S. Marie Oueris,
35 S. Georges,
36 S. Olaves,
37 y. Abby
38 Winchester house,
39 Bankes side,

40 Beare garden
41 Deadmans place,
42 Horsy downe,
43 Artilery Yard,
44 Savory dock,
45 Battle bridge,

◀ On Sunday morning, the wind blew the fire along the north bank of the River Thames.

Samuel Pepys lived several streets from Pudding Lane. His maid told him about the fire during the night. He became worried when he saw the flames on Sunday morning:

"I did see the houses at that end of the bridge all on fire, and an infinite great fire on this and the other side the end of the bridge."

Samuel Pepys

Samuel Pepys

FIGHTING THE FIRE

The Lord Mayor, Sir Thomas Bludworth, had been woken up when officials realized how serious the fire was. They begged him to allow them to demolish houses to stop the fire spreading. If this action had been taken, it might have saved most of London, but Bludworth refused because he was worried about being sued by angry landlords for destroying their properties.

◀ A fire squirt held about as much water as today's large milk cartons.

The buckets and fire squirts that each parish kept for fire fighting were powerless to slow the fire's progress. A fire squirt could hold just two litres of water. Scoops were also used to pile earth on the fire to try to put it out. Samuel Pepys and others noticed that people soon gave up trying to fight the fierce blaze. Instead, they tried to save themselves and their belongings.

Fire engine failure

The new fire engines did not help much. Most had no wheels and were on sleds instead, which made them very difficult to move around the city. They could not even fit down Pudding Lane to get close to the fire. Some fire engines even fell into the River Thames while desperate Londoners tried to fill them up with water.

Charles II

▶ The inaction of the Lord Mayor would force King Charles to get involved in directing the fire fighters.

Fire facts

Fragments of melted pottery from 1666 have been discovered in the area of Pudding Lane. The fragments show that the heat of the fire was more than 1,700° Centigrade (3,092° Fahrenheit), which is hot enough to melt stone.

▲ *Fires need air to burn and throwing earth on the fire could stop the air from reaching it.*

▲ This picture shows how long fire hooks were used to pull down wooden buildings [to st]op fires from spreading.

AN ARCH OF FLAME

Samuel Pepys boarded a boat to inspect the fire from the river. He was amazed to see the speed at which the fire was spreading. Pepys went straight to Whitehall to see the king.

King Charles asked Pepys to try and convince the Lord Mayor to start pulling down houses to stop the fire. Later that same day, the king himself sailed down to the city to give the order to start pulling down buildings. But did the order come too late to stop the fire spreading beyond the waterfront?

Sparks flying

Once the fire had taken hold, it became so fierce that even pulling down buildings could not stop it. The wind carried hot sparks across the city. These sparks set fire to buildings such as the Church of St Lawrence Pountney, which seemed to be far from the flames. People who saw these isolated fires began to suspect that the fires had been started on purpose.

By midday on Sunday, Lord Mayor Bludworth was in despair:

"I have been pulling down houses, but the fire overtakes us faster than we can do it."

▲ *There was no official information about the fire and how it had started. Rumours of foul play started to spread.*

Ciuitatis Westmonasteriensis pars

Parliment House   the Hall   the Abby

▲ The King's palace at Westminster was safe for now but it would be in danger if the fire continued to spread.

As night fell on the burning city, Samuel Pepys and his wife watched the flames from an inn across the river in Southwark:

"We saw the fire as only one entire arch of fire from this to the other side [of] the bridge, and in a bow up the hill for an arch of above a mile long: it made me weep to see it."

▲ This engraving shows the huge area covered by the fire, although it would not all have been burning at once.

SAVE WHAT YOU CAN!

Anyone who was trying to move about the city and fight the fire had to get past the crowds of people running from the flames. The fleeing Londoners carried whatever they could save. Carts, homeless families camping in the streets and huge crowds of scared people clogged up the narrow roads and alleyways.

◀ Most ordinary people had few belongings and could fit everything into a large trunk.

The sick and old who could not escape on their own were carried through the streets on their beds. They did not know if their homes would still be standing when they returned to the city.

Searching for safe places

Londoners piled all kinds of valuables into boats where they would be safe from the fire. In desperation, large wooden trunks and some furniture were thrown directly into the river.

Churches filled up with all kinds of goods. Merchants, traders, and ordinary people thought these solid stone buildings would be safe from the fire. However, the piles of belongings just provided more fuel for the fire as flames swept through the city, cracking and blackening the churches' stone walls.

▲ Musical instruments like t[he?] virginal were valuable. Many [were] thrown into the river to save

▲ The river was crowded with small boats as people tried to save themselves.

◀ The steps down to the river towards the safety of a boat were crowded with people.

On 3 September 1666, John Evelyn wrote in his diary that the River Thames was

"covered with goods floating, all the barges and boats laden with what some had time and courage to save."

SAMUEL PEPYS AND THE FIRE

The story of the fire's unstoppable march across London is told in the diary of Samuel Pepys. Pepys was an important navy official in 1666. He lived in Seething Lane, just a few streets away from where the fire started.

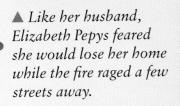

▲ *Like her husband, Elizabeth Pepys feared she would lose her home while the fire raged a few streets away.*

After visiting the king to warn him about the emergency on Sunday, Pepys became worried about his own safety as the fire came closer. He moved his valuables to a friend's house outside the city, and buried some in his garden.

Although his house survived the fire, Pepys and his wife had nightmares about the terrible days when London burned.

On Tuesday 4 September 1666, after the fire had been raging for three days, Pepys buried some wine and cheese that he had not taken to safety:

"Sir W. Pen and I did dig another [pit], and put our wine in it; and I my Parmesan cheese."

Parmesan cheese had to come from Italy, and would have been very expensive.

St Olave's Church, which Pepys attended was just on the edge of the area destroyed by fire.

Samuel Pepys wrote his diary from 1660 to 1669. Much of it was written in code and was only translated more than 150 years later. The diary is one of the most detailed accounts of the Great Fire.

Pepys believed the city could have been saved if the fire had been contained sooner, as he wrote in a letter to his father on the same day:

"The fire is now very near us . . . and we little hope of our escape but by this remedy, to the want whereof we do certainly owe the loss of the City namely, the pulling down of houses, in the way of the fire."

Samuel Pepys

LONDON'S LANDMARKS IN FLAMES

As the fire swept across London, it destroyed much more than people's homes and businesses. On Monday 3 September 1666, the flames spread north, away from the river. London's fashionable streets and famous buildings were soon under threat. It even seemed as if the fire might threaten the Royal Palace and government at Westminster.

▶ James, Duke of York fought bravely over several days to control the fire. He later became King James II.

James

No letters from London

Not many buildings were more important than the General Letter Office. Letters were the only way of getting news and information to and from the rest of the country. When fire struck the letter office, no letters could be sent and London was cut off. The chief clerk James Hicks was the last to leave, carrying as many letters as he could.

By Monday afternoon, the fire had reached the Royal Exchange on Cornhill, the most important place for commerce and trade. And by Tuesday, flames had reached the Guildhall, the home of the city's government. Although its stone walls survived, the inside was gutted by fire.

▶ By Monday, King Charles had taken charge of fighting the fire. Official orders were marked with his Great Seal.

▼ These families are sheltering from the heat of the flames under London Bridge.

Losing the fight

The burning of the city's great buildings proved that the fight against the fire was not working. The king's brother, James, Duke of York, was given the job of organizing teams of fire fighters to create firebreaks across the city. They did this by pulling down yet more buildings. However, they soon found themselves overtaken by the flames as the wind carried sparks across the firebreaks to start new fires on the other side.

▲ Many Londoners were more interested in saving themselves than helping to fight the fire.

THE BURNING OF ST PAUL'S

The greatest landmark of all was St Paul's Cathedral. The cathedral had stood on the highest point of the city for more than 1,000 years. Visitors to London would see it as they sailed up the river. Only as they got closer would they see that parts of the great building were in disrepair and falling down, even before the fire.

Fire facts

The burning of St Paul's was a disaster for printers and booksellers, who lost at least £150,000 worth of precious books. In today's money, that would be more than £11 million pounds.

By Tuesday 4 September 1666, the fire surrounded the cathedral. People still hoped it would survive as it stood apart from other buildings. The printers and booksellers in the streets around the Cathedral believed their books and papers would be safest inside St Paul's. They were all wrong.

▶ *Londoners wondered if the cathedral would ever rise from the ruins.*

Hot metal

As night fell on Tuesday, the first flames were seen on the roof of St Paul's. The books and papers packed into the cathedral ensured that, once the building was alight, it lit up the sky like a giant lantern. As St Paul's burned, the lead on its roof melted and ran down the streets. No fire fighters could cross the red-hot metal.

◀ *In 1666, books were rare and valuable.*

Etiam periere Ruinæ

▶ Once the flames took hold, the books and other goods inside St Paul's fuelled the fire.

FLEEING THE FLAMES

There were no radios or televisions to spread the news of the fire. Even newspaper reports were hardly needed, as the huge cloud of smoke over the city told the story of London's destruction. The glow of the fire could even be seen 80 kilometres (50 miles) away in Oxford. Further away, people were confused as letters and news did not arrive as normal. Many people thought England was being attacked.

Safety in the suburbs

Rich and poor alike had to flee the city. Some crossed the river and watched the flames from Southwark. Others travelled out of the city to places such as Islington and Clerkenwell. Today, these are busy parts of London. In 1666 they were home to grazing animals and windmills.

Around 100,000 people were forced out of the city by the fire. Some had large piles of belongings; others only had the clothes they stood up in. They could only stand and watch as the flames turned everything they owned to ashes.

▲ *Thousands of refugees watched the flames from hills and fields around London.*

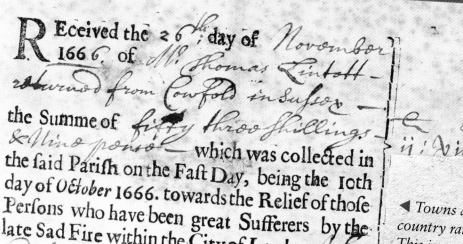

R Eceived the 26th day of November 1666. of Mr Thomas Lintott returned from Cowfold in Sussex the Summe of *fifty three shillings & nine pence* which was collected in the said Parish on the Fast Day, being the 10th day of October 1666. towards the Relief of those Persons who have been great Sufferers by the late Sad Fire within the City of London. Pay'd by order of the Lord Major. Sa. Kendall

£	s	d
ii	viii	iii

◀ Towns and villages across the country raised money for fire refugees. This is a receipt for money raised by the village of Cowfold in Sussex.

His Majestie's
DECLARATION
To His City of
LONDON,
Upon occasion of the late Calamity by the lamentable
FIRE.

DIEV · ET · MON · DROIT

LONDON,
Printed by *John Bill* and *Christopher Barker* Printers to the KING'S most Excellent Majesty, 1666.

CVM PRIVILEGIO.

---

(5)   127

ticular designes must conform themselves. In the first place the woful experience in this late heavy visitation hath sufficiently convinced all men of the pernicious consequences which have attended the building with Timber, and even with Stone it self, and the notable benefit of Brick, which in so many places hath resisted and even extinguished the Fire; And we do therefore hereby declare Our express Wil and Pleasure, That no man whatsoever shal presume to erect any House or Building, great or smal, but of Brick, or Stone, and if any man shal do the contrary, the next Magistrate shal forthwith cause it to be pulled down, and such further course shal be taken for his punishment as he deserves; And We suppose that the notable benefit many men have received from those Cellars which have been wel and strongly arched, wil perswade most men who build good Houses, to practice that good husbandry, by Arching all convenient places.

We do declare, That *Fleetstreet*, *Cheapside*, *Cornhill*, and all other eminent and notorious Streets, shal be of such a breadth, as may with Gods blessing prevent the mischief that one side may suffer if the other be on fire, which was the case lately in *Cheapside*, the precise breadth of which several Streets, shal be upon advice with the Lord Mayor and Al

▲ This document is an order from the King to set up markets so refugees could buy food in the areas outside the city.

HEROES AND CRIMINALS

The fire brought out the best in some people and the worst in others. King Charles II and his brother gained new respect from the people. The King travelled through London on his horse giving money to ordinary people who were battling against the blaze.

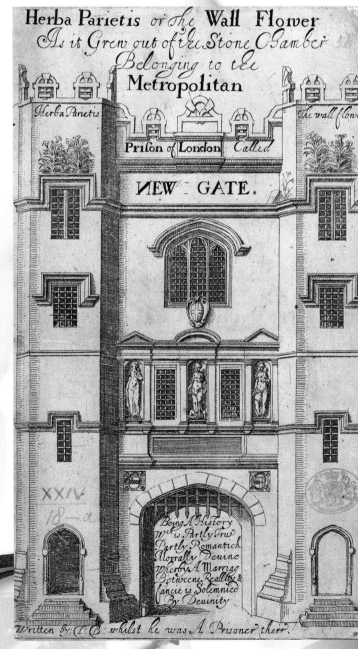

▲ Leather fire helmets like this would have been part of the fire equipment stored in each parish.

Even schoolboys helped in the fight. The boys of Westminster School fought bravely to save the Church of St Dunstan-in-the-East, which was close to Pudding Lane. Despite their best efforts, they were not able to prevent the flames from tearing through the church.

Thieves and looters

The confusion of the fire was a perfect cover for London's criminals. Empty houses were looted and thieves roamed the camps outside the city walls. If they were caught, punishment was harsh. Thieves could be hanged for stealing anything worth more than a shilling (12 pence). Confusion caused by the fire, and the lack of any police force, meant that most criminals were not caught.

▶ Many criminals escaped from prisons. Newgate Prison was deserted by its guards before being destroyed by the fire.

Herba Parietis or the Wall Flower
As it Grew out of the Stone Chamber
Belonging to the
Metropolitan

Herba Parietis

Prison of London Called

The wall flower

NEW GATE.

XXIV
18—a

Being A History
Wch is Partly True
Partly Romantick
Morrally Devine
wherby A Marriag
Betweene Reallity &
Fancie is Solemnico
By Devinity

Written by: C. B: whilst he was A Prisoner their.

A few days after the fire, the king asked thieves to return stolen goods and promised they would not be punished:

"All persons whatsoever who have seized or possessed any plate jewels, money, household stuff, goods or merchandize . . . not truly and of right belonging to them, that they do within the space of eight days after . . . cause the same to be brought into the armoury in Finsbury fields

No one knows how many stolen possessions were actually returned.

▼ Rich people like Samuel Pepys kept their money hidden at home, so there were rich pickings for thieves.

▼ In the confusion of the fire, there were many opportunities for thieves and looters.

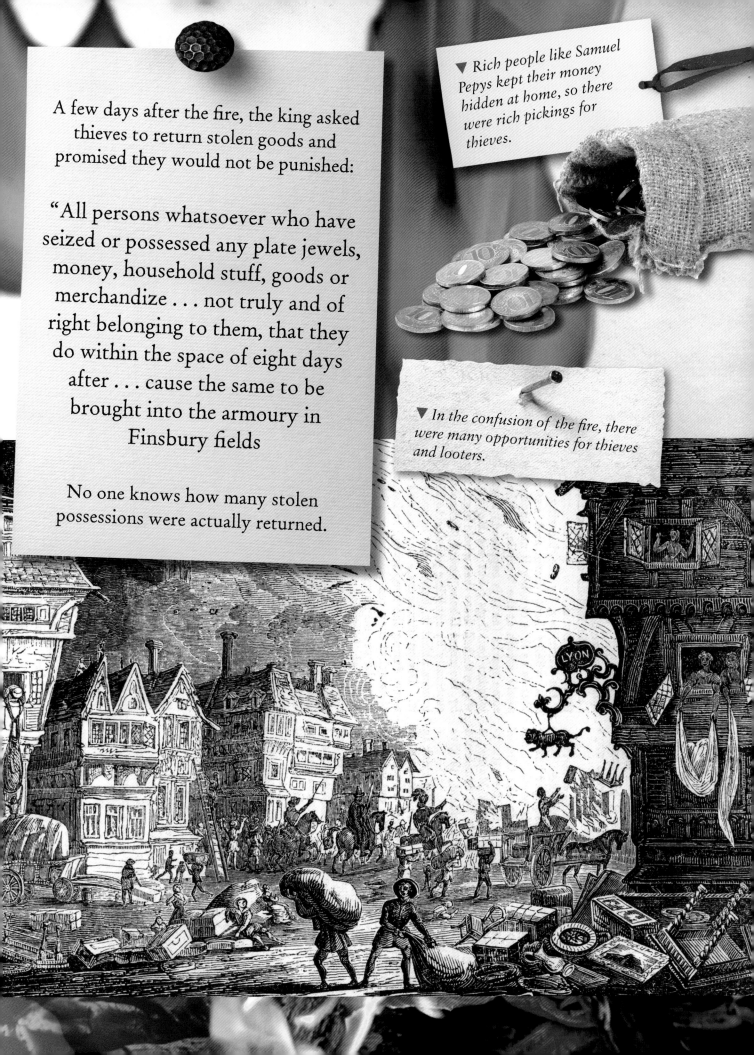

DESPERATE MEASURES

On Tuesday evening, the city was shaken by several huge explosions. Londoners feared that the fire had finally reached the Tower of London and its stock of gunpowder. In fact, the explosions had been set off on purpose in order to destroy buildings around the Tower, stopping the fire from reaching London's gunpowder-packed fortress.

By this time, the fire fighters were exhausted. But as the wind that had fanned the flames started to die down, they finally began to believe that the fire could be beaten.

Protecting Westminster

However, the fire was not finished yet. Now it was threatening Westminster. In a desperate attempt to save the Royal Palace and the houses of the rich, every man, woman, and child was ordered to join in the battle against the fire.

At the same time, the fire was still spreading in the east of the city. Samuel and Elizabeth Pepys awoke at two o'clock in the morning hearing shouts of "Fire!" nearby. They gathered all their money, left immediately and headed downriver by boat, away from the burning city.

Fire facts

Nowadays, people have insurance to pay for rebuilding if their homes or businesses are destroyed by fire. In 1666 no one had fire insurance. The first fire insurance company in London was set up by Nicholas Barbon in 1680.

▲ Nicholas Barbon made himself very rich in helping to rebuild London after the fire.

· GUNPOWDER·

◀ Gunpowder was a more efficient way of demolishing buildings than the old fire hooks.

▼ When the fire reached Ludgate, it threatened the houses of the wealthy to the west of the city.

A TERRIBLE SIGHT

By the afternoon of Wednesday 5 September 1666, the fire fighters were finally sure that they were winning the battle. There were many fires still burning but the wind had dropped. Over the days that followed, new fires flared up in places on the edge of the city, but the Great Fire was finally over.

When it became clear that his house was safe, Pepys climbed to the top of a church tower and saw the city in ruins. The fire had burned almost as far as the Tower of London in the east. In the west it had raged down Fleet Street before being stopped.

Counting the cost

Four-fifths of the city of London had been destroyed. This included 13,200 houses and 87 parish churches. The cost of the fire was put at £10 million pounds, which would be more than 100 times greater in today's money. The real cost was probably much greater, as trade and business was disrupted across the whole of England.

Each of the houses that were destroyed in the fire was a home for at least one family. In poorer areas, many families would have lived in the same house. What would happen to them now?

▲ *Many London businesses were forced to move or close, from the largest companies to street traders like this orange seller.*

▼ This is one of the few city churches to have survived the fire.

Fire facts

Amazingly, official records show that only six people died in the Great Fire of London. It is likely that the real figure was higher as some deaths were not reported or recorded. It would also have been almost impossible to identify the remains of any bodies after the fire.

▶ Fleet Street linked the cities of London and Westminster.

▼ The stone towers of churches stood out above the rubble of the city, as shown in this view of the ruins by Wenceslaus Hollar.

PICKING UP THE PIECES

For thousands of people camped in fields and suburbs around the city, there would be no quick return to their homes in London. Houses could not be rebuilt overnight. The smoking timbers and crumbling stone buildings left by the fire would have to be cleared before anyone could start to rebuild.

▶ People began to return to the city, not even knowing if their homes were still standing.

▲ General George Monck, Duke of Albemarle, was Captain-General of England.

Landlords who owned houses that had escaped the fire found they could charge much higher rents to rich people who had become homeless. People who didn't have any money were left on the streets. With thousands of people with no homes, money, or food, the government was worried that people would start to riot.

Keeping order

Soldiers were ordered into the city. They were led by Sir George Monck, the Duke of Albemarle. The government said that the troops were there to clean up after the fire, but stopping riots was just as important.

THE RIVER THA...MES

...Part of...warke

▲ This map was drawn just after the fire. It shows how much of the city was destroyed.

Fire facts

A fund was set up to help those who had lost everything, but unfortunately it could not help much. Elizabeth Peacock needed £800 to rebuild her house. She only received £10 from the fund.

One writer of the time summed up the fate of the refugees:

"Those that delighted themselves in down beds and silken curtains, are now glad of the shelter of a hedge."

A FOREIGN PLOT?

Long before the fire was brought under control, scared and angry Londoners were looking for someone to blame. England was at war with the Dutch, and tensions were also high between England, which was a Protestant country at the time, and the Catholic countries of France and Spain.

Some English people began to accuse Dutch or French agents of starting the fire. Protestants also accused English Catholics in London of helping the foreigners with their plot. Others blamed God, who had punished London's many sins with war, plague, and now fire.

No one was safe

Violent mobs began roaming the streets, attacking foreigners and their businesses. No one was safe if they were thought to be foreign or Catholic. The Spanish ambassador, Count de Molena, sheltered many foreign and Catholic people in his house to protect them from the angry Londoners.

▲ Europe in the 1600s was divided between the Catholic and Protestant versions of Christianity.

▼ Although England was at war with the Netherlands, many Dutch people lived in London.

▲ *This book blamed Catholics for the fire, although the King himself said that the disaster was an accident.*

Innocent victim

The rumours seemed to be true when Frenchman Robert Hubert confessed to starting the fire. He was executed for this crime. A ship's captain later told a court that he had brought Hubert to London two days after the fire had started. Hubert was an innocent man.

An official report into the cause of the fire accused foreigners and Catholics, but included no real evidence. The king and his advisers concluded that the fire was caused by "the hand of God" and the dry, windy weather that spread the flames.

▶ *Robert Hubert claimed that he had thrown a fireball through the window of Farriner's bakery in Pudding Lane.*

A LUCKY ESCAPE

Damage from the fire was terrible. The city took many years to rebuild, but things could have been much worse. Most amazing of all was the small number of people who died in the fire. How did so many thousands of people escape?

▲ *Paper records of businesses and who owned them were lost forever because of the Great Fire.*

Londoners were well used to fires. Most people had plenty of warning that the fire was coming and had time to leave their houses. They knew how quickly fires could spread and that buildings could collapse. They got out of the way as fast as they could.

Business as usual

In the weeks after the fire, some businesses were quick to return to the city. The Royal Exchange started using another building on the edge of the city. James Hicks reopened the General Letter Office in an inn until another building could be found.

Many other Londoners found it much harder to recover from the fire. Some moved to other cities to start a new life. For those who stayed, the task of rebuilding London was long and hard.

▲ *This sermon was printed to mark a fast day that was declared to remember the fire and help raise money for the victims.*

▶ *Humphrey Henchman, the Bishop of London, insisted that booksellers and other businesses around St Paul's should still pay their rent even though their buildings were in ruins.*

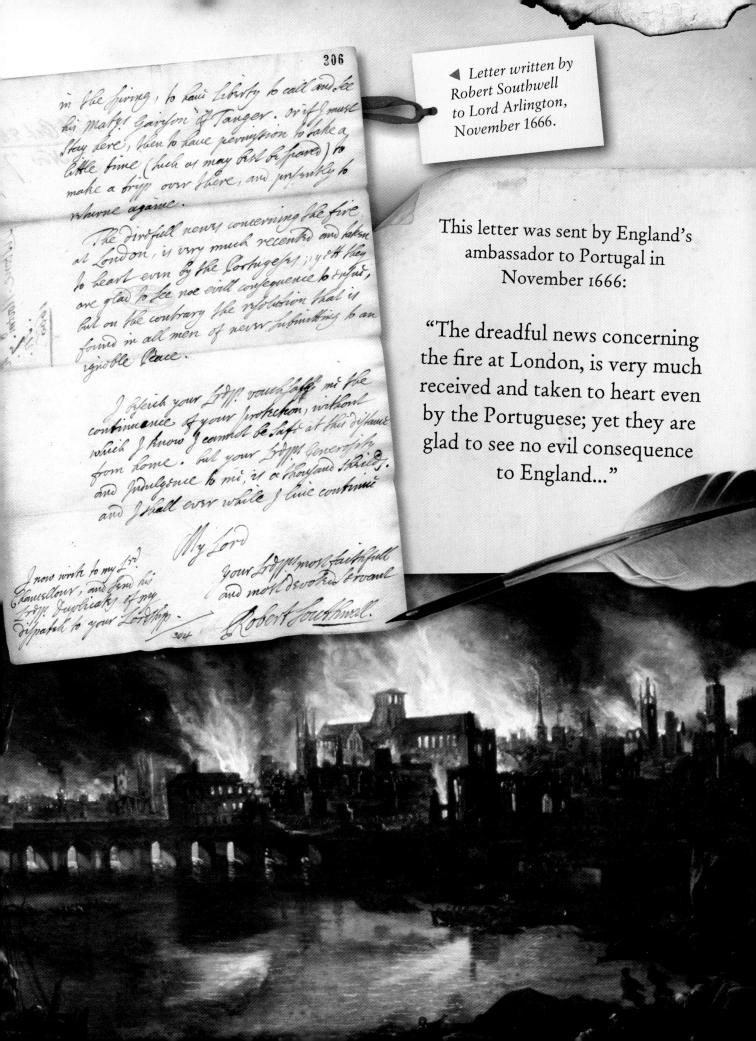

in the firing, to have liberty to call and see his Maty.s Garyson of Tanger. or if I must stay here, then to have permission to take a little time (such as may best be spared) to make a tryp over there, and presently to returne againe.

The dirdfull news concerning the fire at London, is very much recented and taken to heart even by the Portugess; yett they are glad to see noe evill consequence to ensue, but on the contrary the resolution that is found in all men of never submitting to an ignoble Peace.

I beseich your Lordp. vouchsaffe me the continuance of your protection, without which I know I cannot be safe at this distance from home. but your Lordp.s Generosity and Indulgence to me, is a thousand shields, and I shall ever while I live continue

My Lord

I now write to my Lord Chancellour, and send his Lordp. duplicats of my dispatch to your Lordshipp.

Your Lordp.s most faithfull and most devoted servant

Robert Southwell.

304

Letter written by Robert Southwell to Lord Arlington, November 1666.

This letter was sent by England's ambassador to Portugal in November 1666:

"The dreadful news concerning the fire at London, is very much received and taken to heart even by the Portuguese; yet they are glad to see no evil consequence to England..."

NEVER AGAIN

The first task of the king and the government was to make sure that London could never again be faced with such a calamity. The narrow alleys and overhanging wooden buildings of old London had helped the fire spread. These buildings would no longer be allowed. All new buildings had to be built of brick or stone.

▲ *This tavern sign is dated 1670. Inns and taverns were built for the workers rebuilding the city.*

▼ *The fire destroyed most of London's wooden buildings.*

Fire rules

The city was split into four sections to fight future fires. Each had fire equipment including 800 buckets. The city's watch had to walk the streets at night looking for fires. Fireplaces also had to be inspected twice a year to make sure they were safe.

There was still no fire brigade for London. The first organized fire services were paid for by insurance companies after 1680, when London's new buildings started to be insured against fire.

◀ *Fire buckets were lined with pitch to make them waterproof. Buckets needed to be maintained so they did not split.*

◀ In February 1667 a Rebuilding Act laid down rules on new buildings and even the thickness of the new brick walls.

A few days after the fire, the king sent out a proclamation containing rules for rebuilding the city:

All buildings were to be made of stone or brick

Main streets should be wide enough that fire could not spread from one side to the other

Narrow lanes and alleys should only be allowed if the city decided they were really needed

No houses were to be built next to the river

City officials should decide on a place where all trades that used fires for their work could be housed together.

His Majestie's
DECLARATION
To His City of
LONDON,
Upon occasion of the late Calamity by the lamentable
FIRE.

DIEV · ET · MON DROIT

LONDON,
Printed by John Bill and Christopher Barker Printers to the KING'S most Excellent Majesty, 1666.

CUM PRIVILEGIO.

▲ The King's declaration on rebuilding London laid the foundations of a new city.

▶ Narrow alleys such as the ones leading to the river were to be widened.

PLANNING A NEW CITY

The fire had been a disaster, but some of London's most important people saw it as a chance to build a wonderful new city. England's greatest scholars set to work on grand plans for the "new" London. They wanted to match the squares and wide avenues of Paris and Rome. They believed London could become the greatest city in Europe.

John Evelyn produced three plans in total. His ideas included wide, straight streets and circular piazzas that were very different from the winding, jumbled streets of London before the fire.

Robert Hooke made amazing discoveries in many areas of science before turning to city planning in 1666. His plan was preferred by the city authorities. Evelyn wrote that "everyone brings in his idea", and many other plans were produced. Captain Valentine Knight's design even included a wide canal that snaked through the streets of London.

Robert Hooke

A burned wasteland

While the king and the city government argued over the different plans and cleared the ruins of the fire, the burnt area of London became a wasteland. It was filled with hovels and shacks built by homeless Londoners. The ruins were also home to criminals.

▶ *John Evelyn's plan for rebuilding his city.*

▶ *Samuel Pepys carried a sword when walking through the rubble-covered streets at night.*

Gründtriß der Statt LONDON, wie solche vor und nach dem Brand anzusehen sampt dem Newen Model, wie selbige widrum Auffgebauwet werden solle

Model, wie die Abgebrante Statt LONDON, widrum Auffgebauwet werden solle

▼ Robert Hooke's plan for London is shown at the bottom of this map.

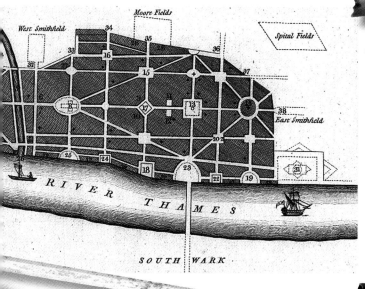

Fire facts

Captain Valentine Knight claimed that his plan for rebuilding London would make lots of money for the royal household. King Charles II was offended by this suggestion, and had him arrested.

SIR CHRISTOPHER WREN'S MASTERPIECE

One of the first people to present his new plan to the king was Christopher Wren. Wren was actually Professor of Astronomy at Oxford University as well as an architect. His ambitious plan for London was never built, but Wren played a big part in deciding what the new city would look like.

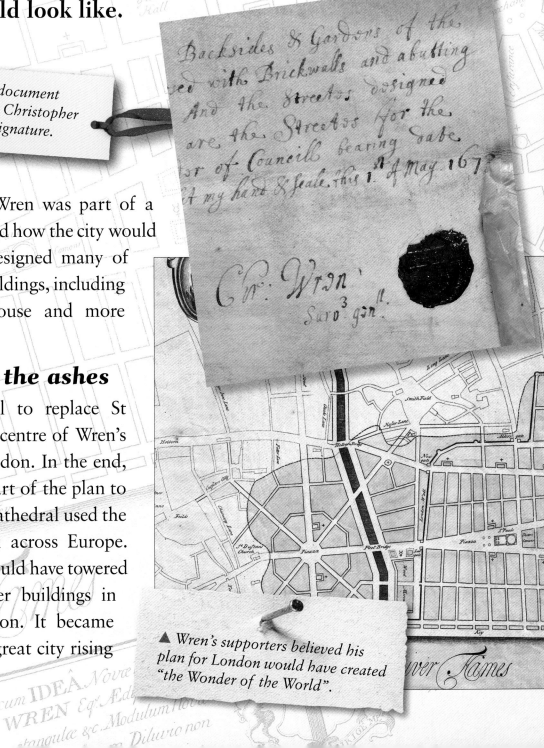

▶ This document includes Christopher Wren's signature.

From the start, Wren was part of a group who decided how the city would be rebuilt. He designed many of London's new buildings, including the Customs House and more than 50 churches.

Rising from the ashes

A new cathedral to replace St Paul's was at the centre of Wren's first plan for London. In the end, it was the only part of the plan to be built. Wren's cathedral used the latest ideas from across Europe. Its giant dome would have towered over all the other buildings in the "new" London. It became the symbol of a great city rising from the ashes.

▲ Wren's supporters believed his plan for London would have created "the Wonder of the World".

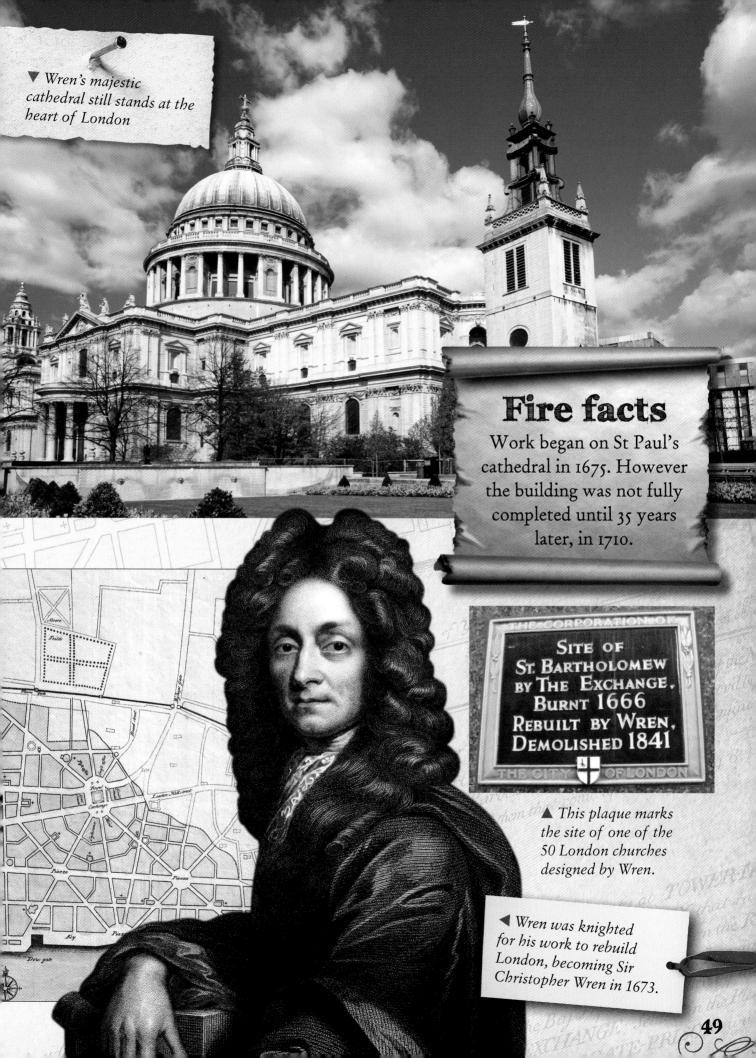

▼ Wren's majestic cathedral still stands at the heart of London

Fire facts

Work began on St Paul's cathedral in 1675. However the building was not fully completed until 35 years later, in 1710.

THE CORPORATION OF

SITE OF
ST. BARTHOLOMEW
BY THE EXCHANGE,
BURNT 1666
REBUILT BY WREN,
DEMOLISHED 1841

THE CITY OF LONDON

▲ This plaque marks the site of one of the 50 London churches designed by Wren.

◀ Wren was knighted for his work to rebuild London, becoming Sir Christopher Wren in 1673.

REBUILDING LONDON

Everyone soon realized that all the grand plans for London would be far too difficult to build. People who had owned houses in the city simply wanted to rebuild them in the same place. Some streets were widened but the plan of streets in the city did not change too much as the new stone and brick buildings sprung up.

Settling disputes

Before a house could be rebuilt, surveyors had to confirm who owned the land and mark it out. There were many cases of people moving these markers at night to make their plot of land bigger. Most buildings were rented and there were disputes about whether landlords or tenants should pay for rebuilding.

If people disagreed about land and who should pay for rebuilding, the case would be decided by special "fire courts". This helped to speed up the process of creating the new city.

Fire facts

After the Great Plague of 1665, the plague never returned to London. Some people believe that the Great Fire helped London to stay plague-free. The new rules about building brick houses and wider roads meant that parts of London were much less cramped and dirty. This also meant that many Londoners had less contact with rats and fleas. However, no one really knows the truth about why the disease never came back.

▶ Fire courts operated for five years to settle all disputes after the fire.

This painting shows the stone buildings of the new city in about 1740.

The city reborn

Work began in spring 1667. More than 1,400 houses were built in the first year. Ten years later, most of the city had been rebuilt. Public buildings such as churches were paid for by a new tax on coal. This tax was still in place 200 years later, long after London had been rebuilt.

▶ The tax was collected on coal brought into the port of London.

▲ This map shows how London was rebuilt and growing fast by 1700.

▼ London's first publicly-funded fire service was eventually set up after the Tooley Street fire of 1861.

LOOKING FOR CLUES

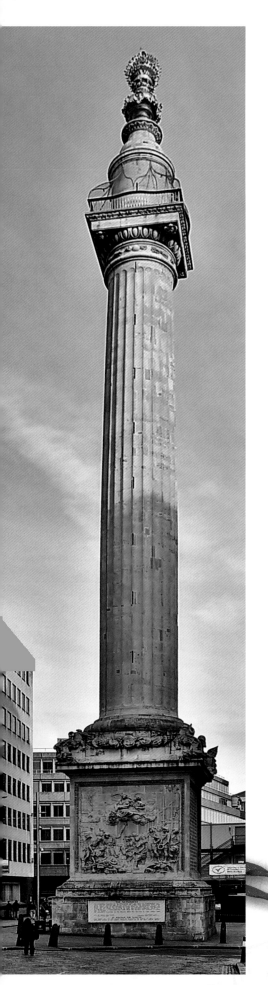

London recovered from the fire. In 1700 it was home to 600,000 people. By 1800, London was the largest and most prosperous city in the world. The huge growth of London means that it can be difficult to find traces of the city that was rebuilt after 1666, let alone the disorderly and chaotic city that existed before the fire.

London Life

Written documents can tell us what it was like to live in London during the Great Fire. The London Gazette from 10 September 1666 gave the first full report on the fire:

"It fell out most unhappily too, that a violent easterly wind . . . kept it burning all that day and the night following spreading itself up to Gracechurch Street and downwards to Cannon Street and the Waterside."

◄ Down a narrow street near London Bridge stands "the Monument". This was designed by Robert Hooke and Christopher Wren and was built close to where the Great Fire started at Thomas Farriner's bakery in Pudding Lane.

▲ The London Gazette was the government's official newspaper. When it failed to appear during the fire, people outside London assumed the city was under attack.

▲ The dome of St Paul's Cathedral today looks much smaller than many of the buildings around it. When it was completed in 1710, it would have stood out high above the houses to show that London was reborn.

▲ Staples Inn in Holborn was built in 1596. It was outside the area destroyed by fire, but shows us what many of London's buildings would have looked like before 1666.

CITIES IN FLAMES

The Great Fire of London was one of the most dramatic events in history, but London was not the last city to be destroyed by fire. Many cities have burned since, either by accident or during wartime.

On 8 October 1871, after a hot, dry summer, a fire started in O'Leary's barn in Chicago in the USA. The story was that a cow had kicked over a lantern. The fire destroyed a third of the city and killed 300 people. In 1906, fire swept through San Francisco on the West Coast of America after an earthquake tipped over burning stoves and broke gas pipes. This fire destroyed four fifths of the city and killed about 3,000 people.

The Second World War, between 1939 and 1945, brought deliberate attacks on cities by aircraft using bombs designed to cause fires. Cities such as Coventry in England and Dresden in Germany suffered from devastating fires caused by air raids.

▲ Oil lamps were a major fire risk before electric lights became popular in the late 1800s.

▼ The fires that swept through San Francisco killed more people than the earthquake that caused them.

The ruins of Chicago in 1871 were replaced by some of the world's first skyscrapers.

American journalist Ernie Pyle's reported on the Blitz on 29 December 1940:

"You have all seen big fires, but I doubt if you have ever seen the whole horizon of a city lined with great fires – scores of them, perhaps hundreds."

This famous picture from the Second World War shows the dome of St Paul's Cathedral surrounded by the smoke of explosions and fires.

The last great fire?

The night of 29 December 1940 was one of several nights when German aircraft attacked London during the Blitz. On that night, more than 1,500 separate fires were started by falling bombs. It was the closest the city had ever come to a repeat of the Great Fire of 1666. Yet once again, London rose from the ashes to become the city we know today.

DEALING WITH DISASTERS

Huge fires like the one that struck London in 1666, and Chicago in 1871, are now part of history. Modern cities are built from bricks and concrete, rather than wooden buildings.

Today's cities are bigger and more complex than the cities of the past. They also face emergencies. These can be caused by extreme weather, such as super-storm Sandy that struck New York City in America in 2012. They can also be caused by wars or attacks by terrorists.

Are we better prepared now?

We have many advantages over the people who battled the Great Fire of London. Every city is now patrolled by fire fighters, who can respond quickly to any outbreaks of fire. In 1666, it took several days for people outside London to find out about the fire. Today, phones and the Internet enable people to respond to emergencies instantly.

▼ *Modern fire fighters use breathing equipment and other technology to help them fight fires.*

Yet we can also learn from the Great Fire of London. The fire spread because people made the wrong choices. Houses were not pulled down to stop the fire before it got out of control. Efforts to put out the fire were disorganised and there was no central control. Even with the best equipment in the world, making the right choices and good organisation are essential to deal with any emergency.

Fire facts

A modern fire hose takes just one-tenth of a second to produce as much water as a fire squirt could hold in 1666.

◀ Motor-powered fire engines were first introduced in the early 1900s. Their sirens are still a familiar sound on city streets.

▼ Huge fires can still burn out of control in dry forests and wilderness areas.

GREAT FIRE TIMELINE

AD60 Boudica's forces burn London to the ground during their revolt against the Roman invaders who built the city.

1212 London is once again destroyed by one of the many fires to hit the city. This fire was known as the "Great Fire" before the fire of 1666.

1660 King Charles II comes to the throne after 20 years of civil war and the government of Oliver Cromwell.

1666

2 September: 1.00 am: Fire breaks out in Thomas Farriner's bakery on Pudding Lane.

4.00 am: Lord Mayor Thomas Bludworth is awoken with news of the fire. He refuses to allow buildings to be destroyed to stop the flames spreading.

7.00 am: Pepys gets out of bed and is told that 300 houses have been destroyed.

3.00 pm: King Charles II travels along the River Thames by boat to see the progress of the fire.

Evening: Samuel Pepys watches the fire from across the river and sees an arch of flame a mile long.

3 September: 1.00 am: The main post office, one of the only ways in which news could spread to and from London, burns down.

9.00 am: James, Duke of York takes charge of fighting the fire, setting up fire crews at different points around the city.

Afternoon: The Royal Exchange, the centre of London trade and business, burns down.

4 September: Morning: Houses are blown up with gunpowder to try and stop the fire reaching the Tower of London where the city's gunpowder stores are kept.

7.00 pm: Pepys and his neighbour bury their wine and Parmesan cheese in case the fire reaches their houses.

8.00 pm: St Paul's Cathedral catches fire, including the many books and other personal belongings stored inside it.

5 September: Morning: The king orders markets to be set up to provide food for thousands of refugees outside the city. The wind starts to drop and the fire's progress is stopped in the west of the city, although fires still burn across the rest of London.

6 September: 5.00 am: The last outbreak of fire is battled at Bishopsgate. By now, the fire has destroyed 13,200 houses.

Morning: The King reassures crowds outside the city that the Great Fire was an accident and not a foreign plot.

11 September: Christopher Wren presents his plan to rebuild the city.

27 October: Frenchman Robert Hubert is executed for confessing to starting the fire. He was almost certainly innocent of the crime, as he did not arrive in London until two days after the fire started.

1675

Work begins on building Christopher Wren's domed St Paul's Cathedral.

1680 The first fire insurance company is set up in London.

1700 London is now home to 600,000 people, almost twice as many people as lived there before the Great Fire of 1666.

1710 The rebuilding of St Paul's Cathedral is completed.

1871 8 October: Fire starts in the American city of Chicago, caused by a cow knocking over a lantern. Much of the city is destroyed and many are killed.

1940 29 December: The heaviest attacks of the Blitz on London during the Second World War take place, starting more than 1,500 fires.

GLOSSARY

ambitious trying to achieve a high standard or a difficult goal

air raid attack by aircraft dropping bombs on to a city or other target

architect person who designs buildings

astrologer person who claims to tell the future from movements of the stars and planets across the night sky

ballad poem or song that tells a story

Catholic Christian who is a member of the Roman Catholic Church, led by the Pope

cellar room or part of a building below ground level

civil war conflict between two sides from the same country, such as the conflict between forces of the King and parliament in the English Civil War

compensation money paid to make up for the loss of something, such as for losses caused by the Great Fire

Dutch name for people from the Netherlands

evidence information that can help to prove something, such as whether a person has committed a crime

executed when a person is killed on the orders of a court because they have been found guilty of a crime

fire break area where buildings or other materials are removed to stop the progress of a fire

gunpowder mix of materials that causes explosions

gutted burned from the inside, although the outer walls are still standing

hovels shacks or temporary buildings

insurance agreement in which a regular payment, or premium, is paid so that an insurance company will cover the cost of replacing a building or other valuable item if it is destroyed or stolen

landlord   person who owns a building. People who live there may pay rent to the landlord or landlady

livery company   organizations managing different trades and crafts in the city of London, such as the companies of grocers, drapers (cloth merchants), or fishmongers

Lord Mayor   person who, in 1666, was the leading official in the city of London and is still elected by the city's livery companies

pamphlet   small book without a hard cover or binding

parish   area of a town or country organized around a church

piazza   grand public square or marketplace, often found in European cities

proclamation   official document or announcement

prosperous   rich or successful

Protestant   Christian who is a member of any of the churches that broke away from the Roman Catholic Church from the 1500s onwards

rent   money paid to a landlord by a tenant for use of a property

riot   public disturbance during which people or properties are attacked

scholar   learned person

suburb   area outside the centre of a city

tenant   someone who pays rent on a property to someone else

terrorist   person or group of people who use violence against ordinary people to achieve a political goal

Find Out More

Books

The Great Fire of London (Historical Stories)
by Jill Atkins (Wayland, 2008)
Fictional retelling of the Great Fire, based on real historical characters.

Plague Unclassified: Secrets of the Great Plague Revealed (The National Archives)
Find out more about London in 1665, the plague-infested year before the Great Fire   (A & C Black, 2013)

Plague: A Cross on the Door and The Great Fire: A City in Flames (The National Archives)
Two-part story about a young Londoner, Sam, and his battle to survive the deadly plague, followed by the worst fire in London's history.
by Ann Turnbull (A & C Black, 2013)

Avoid Being in the Great Fire of London (The Danger Zone series)
by Jim Pipe and David Antram (Book House, 2010)

See Inside London by Rob Lloyd Jones (Usborne, 2007)
Includes a section about London during the fire.

Online resources

See if you can help two Londoners survive the Great Fire in this free online game.
www.fireoflondon.org.uk/game

The Museum of London is a great place to discover more about the Great Fire and the whole history of London. You may be able to visit the museum but, if not, the 'London's Burning' website contains lots of information on the Great Fire.
www.museumoflondon.org.uk/Explore-online/Past/LondonsBurning/

Find out more about the history of fire fighting at the London Fire Brigade Museum.
www.london-fire.gov.uk/OurMuseum.asp

Samuel Pepys is an important figure from the time of the Great Fire. This BBC website tells his life story for younger readers.
www.bbc.co.uk/schools/famouspeople/standard/pepys/index.shtml#focus

You can read the full entries from Samuel Pepys' diary about the Great Fire here:
www.pepysdiary.com/diary/1666/09/

Discover more about the monument that was built to mark the Great Fire and still stands in London today. **www.themonument.info**

The National Archives

The National Archives is the UK government's official archive containing over 1,000 years of history. They give detailed guidance to government departments and the public sector on information management, and advise others about the care of historical archives.
www.nationalarchives.gov.uk

National Archives picture acknowledgements and catalogue references

p2, p48 MPA1/22. Christopher Wren's signature. p3, p26 SP108.388. Great Seal of Charles II. p15 E 179/252/32/4. Hearth tax return. p17, p25 PROB 1/9. Samuel Pepys signature. p31, p45 SP 29/171. The King's Declaration

Picture Acknowledgements

Front cover images: Background ZMAP4_18 © The National Archives, all montage images Shutterstock and Wikimeda. Back cover images: Background ZMAP4_18 © The National Archives, all montage images Shutterstock and Wikimeda aside from, Hulton Archive/Getty Images.
Inside images all Shutterstock, aside from the following: p4 bottom Wenceslas Hollar/Wikimedia, p5 bottom Museum of London, p5 top Hendrick Van der Borcht/Wikimedia, p6 bottom Wenceslas Hollar/Wikimedia, p7 top left Wikimedia, p7 top right Hulton Archive/Getty Images, p7 bottom Wenceslas Hollar/Wikimedia, p8 top left Bettmann/Corbis, p8 centre right Wikimedia, p9 Antoon van Dyck/Wikimedia, p9 top and bottom right Museum of London, p10 bottom right koya979/Shutterstock, p11 Universal History Archive/Getty Images, p12 centre Museum of London, p12-13 Wenceslas Hollar/Wikimedia, p13 Keeling/Wikimedia, p14 bottom right Museum of London, p14-15 centre Hulton Archive/Getty Images, p15 top right Popperfoto/Getty Images, p16 bottom Wikimedia, p17 top Wenceslas Hollar/Wikimedia, p17 bottom right Hulton Archive/Getty Images, p18 bottom right Wikimedia, p18 top Museum of London, p19 bottom Wikimedia, p20 bottom left SSPL/Getty Images, p20-21 Museum of London, p21 Wenceslas Hollar/Wikimedia, p22 centre right Gabriël Metsu/Wikimedia, p23 top Museum of London, p23 bottom right Universal History Archive/Getty Images, p24 top left Wikimedia, p24-25 centre-bottom right Wikimedia, p25 top Wikimedia, p26 centre Sir Peter Lely/Wikimedia, p27 top Museum of London, p27 bottom Hulton Archive/Getty Images, p29 top Wenceslas Hollar/Wikimedia, p29 centre Wikimedia, p30 centre Hulton Archive/Getty Images, p31 top Museum of London, p31 bottom Museum of London, p32 top left Museum of London, p32 bottom right Wikimedia, p33 top right Sergey Ksen/Shutterstock, p33 bottom Hulton Archive/Getty Images, p34 centre right Wikimedia, p35 Wikimedia, p36 top right Museum of London, p36-37 Wenceslas Hollar/Wikimedia, p37 top left View Pictures/UIG/Getty Images, p38 top Bettmann/Corbis, p38 bottom left Wikimedia, p39 top Wikimedia, p40 bottom Jan van Leyden/Wikimedia, p41 bottom right Museum of London, p41 top Museum of London, p42 left Hulton Archive/Getty Images, p43 Imagno/Getty Images, p44 top right Museum of London, p44 bottom left Museum of London, p44 bottom right Museum of London, p46 Wikimedia, p47 top Museum of London, p47 bottom Wikimedia, p48-49 centre Wikimedia, p49 top vichie81/Shutterstock, p49 bottom Georgios Kollidas/Shutterstock, p49 bottom right Wikimedia, p50-51 top Museum of London, p51 top right Wikimedia, p51 bottom right Museum of London, p52 left Wikimedia, p52 right Wikimedia p53 top Pawel Libera/Shutterstock, p53 bottom Jim Linwood/Flickr, p54 bottom Wikimedia, p55 top Archive Photos/Getty Images, p55 bottom right Time Life Pictures/New York Times Paris Bureau Collection/National Archives/Time Life Pictures/Getty Images, p56 bottom right Four Oaks/Shutterstock, p57 bottom right Peter J. Wilson/Shutterstock, p58 centre Wikiemdia, p59 top left Wenceslas Hollar/Wikimedia, p59 bottom right

INDEX